RUM

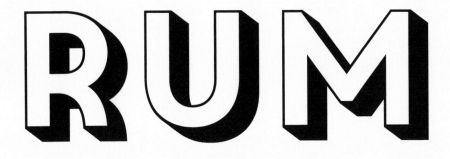

CLASSIC &
CONTEMPORARY
COCKTAILS

An Hachette UK Company
www.hachette.co.uk

First published in Great Britain in 2018 by Hamlyn,
an imprint of Octopus Publishing Group Ltd
Carmelite House, 50 Victoria Embankment, London EC4Y 0DZ
www.octopusbooks.co.uk

Distributed in the US by
Hachette Book Group
1290 Avenue of the Americas
4th and 5th Floors
New York, NY 10104

Distributed in Canada by
Canadian Manda Group
664 Annette St.
Toronto, Ontario, Canada M6S 2C8

ISBN 978-0-75373-330-1

A CIP catalogue record for this book is available from the British Library

Printed and bound in China

10 9 8 7 6 5 4 3 2

Publisher: Lucy Pessell
Designer: Lisa Layton
Editor: Sarah Vaughan
Production Manager: Caroline Alberti
Cover and interior motifs created by: Abhimanyu Bose, LSE Designs, Magicon, Valeriy,
Wuppdidu. All from *The Noun Project*.

The measure that has been used in the recipes is based on a bar jigger, which is 25 ml (1 fl oz).
If preferred, a different volume can be used, providing the proportions are kept constant within a
drink and suitable adjustments are made to spoon measurements, where they occur.

Standard level spoon measurements are used in all recipes.
1 tablespoon = one 15 ml spoon
1 teaspoon = one 5 ml spoon

This book contains cocktails made with raw or lightly cooked eggs. It is prudent for more vulnerable
people to avoid uncooked or lightly cooked cocktails made with eggs.

Some of this material previously appeared in *Hamlyn All Colour Cookery: 200 Classic Cocktails* and
501 Must-Drink Cocktails.

RUM

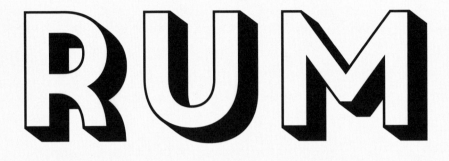

CLASSIC &
CONTEMPORARY
COCKTAILS

hamlyn

CONTENTS

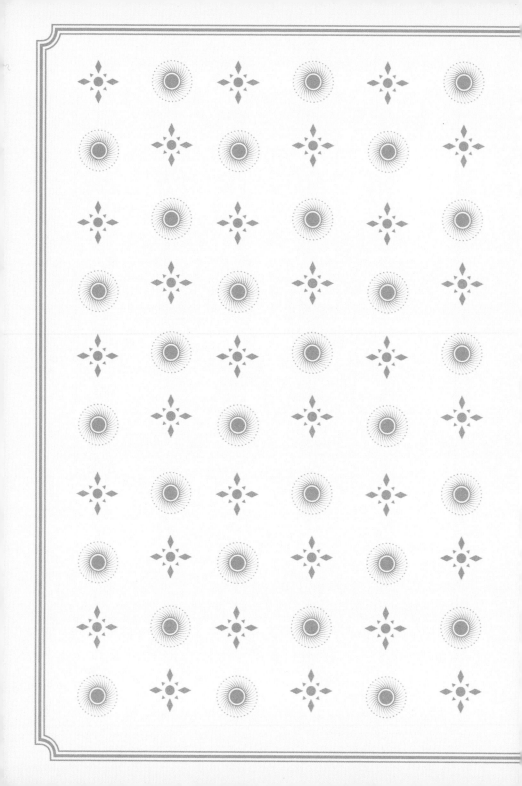

A BRIEF HISTORY OF RUM & COCKTAILS

The origin of the word 'COCKTAIL' is widely disputed.

Initially used to describe the docked tails of horses that were not thoroughbred (which hasn't much to do with a Singapore Sling), the alleged first definition of a 'cocktail' appeared in New York's *The Balance and Columbian Repository*. In response to the question 'What is a cocktail?' the editor replied: 'it is a stimulating liquor, composed of spirits of any kind, sugar, water and bitters... in as much as it renders the heart stout and bold, at the same time that it fuddles the head... because a person, having swallowed a glass of it, is ready to swallow anything else.' Which sounds a little more like it.

However it began, this delightful act of mixing varying amounts of spirits, sugar and bitters has evolved, after decades of fine crafting, experimentation and even 13 years of prohibition in the United States, into the 'cocktail' we know and love. Each one a masterpiece. Each one to be made just right for you.

In the century since Harry Craddock concocted the Corpse Reviver and the White Lady, James Bond has insisted on breaking the number 1 rule to not shake a Martini every time he goes to the bar, and *Sex and the City* has introduced a whole new generation of drinkers to the very pink, very fabulous, Cosmopolitan cocktail. And the idea it can be paired with a burger and fries. Which is fine by us.

Go forth and make yours a Martini. Or a French Afternoon at gin o'clock on a mizzly Monday morning.

RUM is a distilled spirit made from sugarcane and is usually aged in barrels.

Hailing from the Caribbean, it was first distilled on sugarcane plantations back in the 17th century and found its way across the seven seas under all sorts of pseudonyms that give us a pretty good idea of its original tasting notes.

This Nelson's blood, or kill-devil demon water, was imbibed to combat scurvy, warm the cockles and put the irate in pirate. Thankfully, some clever coves recognised it as having the potential to be a jolly good snifter and refined it a little.

Rum now comes in various grades across a honeyed-in-colour and sugar-and-spice-in-flavour spectrum. From light, almost clear, to golden, dark and stormy, it is all caramel, banana, chocolate, ginger, vanilla and cinnamon. Pirates' grog it ain't.

Here's a collection of cocktail recipes with rum at their ar-me-hearty heart. From the sweet-sour, lip-smacking Daiquiri, and the hello sunshine, make mine a Piña Colada, to the garden party favourite Long Island Iced Tea, it's 'Yo-ho-ho and a bottle of rum' and, no, not a bottle. Please, drink responsibly.

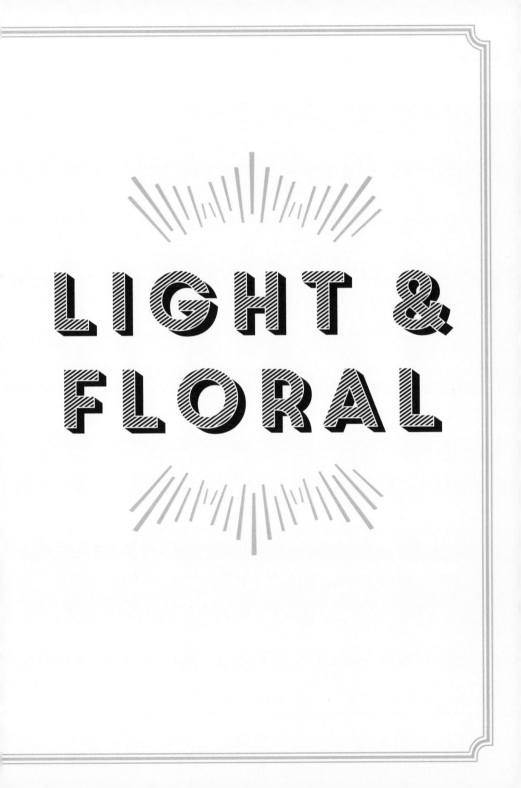

LIGHT & FLORAL

PINEAPPLE MOJITO

2 MEASURES GOLDEN RUM

½ LIME, HALVED

6 MINT LEAVES

4 PINEAPPLE CHUNKS

2 TSP SOFT BROWN SUGAR

PINEAPPLE JUICE, TO TOP

PINEAPPLE & MINT SPRIG, TO GARNISH

Muddle the mint leaves, pineapple chunks, lime and sugar in a cocktail shaker. Add the rum and shake well.

Strain into a highball glass filled with crushed ice, top up with pineapple juice and stir.

Garnish with a pineapple wedge and a mint sprig and serve with straws.

NEW ORLEANS DANDY

1 MEASURE WHITE RUM

½ MEASURE PEACH BRANDY

1 DASH ORANGE JUICE

1 DASH LIME JUICE

CHAMPAGNE, TO TOP

Put some ice cubes into a cocktail shaker and pour the rum, peach brandy and fruit juices over it.

Shake until a frost forms, strain into a Champagne flute or tall glass and top up with Champagne.

HAVANA BEACH

1 MEASURE WHITE RUM

½ LIME

2 MEASURES PINEAPPLE JUICE

1 TSP SUGAR

DRY GINGER ALE, TO TOP

LIME, TO GARNISH

Cut the lime into 4 pieces and put into a food processor or blender with the pineapple juice, rum and sugar. Blend until smooth.

Pour into a hurricane glass or large goblet and top up with ginger ale.

Garnish with a lime slice.

APPLE-SOAKED MOJITO

2 MEASURES GOLDEN RUM

8 MINT LEAVES, PLUS AN EXTRA SPRIG, TO GARNISH

½ LIME, CUT INTO WEDGES

2 TSP SUGAR SYRUP

2 MEASURES GOLDEN RUM

APPLE JUICE, TO TOP

RED APPLE & A CINNAMON STICK, TO GARNISH

Muddle the mint leaves, lime wedges and sugar syrup in a cocktail shaker.

Add the rum, shake well and strain into a highball glass filled with crushed ice.

Top with apple juice and garnish with a mint sprig, cinnamon stick and an apple slice.

AFTER DARK CRUSH

2 MEASURES BARBADIAN RUM

½ MEASURE KOKO KANU (COCONUT RUM)

½ MEASURE VANILLA SYRUP

1 MEASURE COCONUT CREAM

SODA WATER, TO TOP

COCKTAIL CHERRIES, TO GARNISH

Fill a sling glass with crushed ice, then add, one by one, in order, the rums, vanilla syrup and coconut cream.

Stir and top up with soda water.

Add more ice and garnish with cocktail cherries. Serve with long straws.

BLUE HAWAIIAN

1 MEASURE WHITE RUM

½ MEASURE BLUE CURAÇAO

2 MEASURES PINEAPPLE JUICE

1 MEASURE COCONUT CREAM

PINEAPPLE & COCKTAIL CHERRY, TO GARNISH

Put some crushed ice into a food processor or blender and pour in the rum, Curaçao, pineapple juice and coconut cream.

Blend at high speed for 20–30 seconds.

Pour into a chilled cocktail glass and garnish with a pineapple wedge and a cocktail cherry.

BOLERO

1 ½ MEASURES WHITE RUM

¾ MEASURE APPLE BRANDY

SEVERAL DROPS SWEET VERMOUTH

LEMON, TO GARNISH

Put some ice cubes into a cocktail shaker and pour over the rum, apple brandy and vermouth. Shake well.

Strain into a glass and add ice cubes.

Squeeze the zest from a lemon rind twist over the glass and drop it in.

COOPER COOLER

2 MEASURES GOLDEN RUM

3 MEASURES DRY GINGER ALE

1 TBSP LIME OR LEMON JUICE

LIME OR LEMON, TO GARNISH

Put some ice cubes into a highball glass.

Pour over the rum, ginger ale and lime or lemon juice and stir.

Garnish with a lime or lemon slice.

FLORIDA SKIES

1 MEASURE WHITE RUM

¼ MEASURE LIME JUICE

½ MEASURE PINEAPPLE JUICE

SODA WATER, TO TOP UP

CUCUMBER OR LIME, TO GARNISH

Put some cracked ice into a tall glass.

Add the rum and fruit juices into a cocktail shaker. Shake lightly.

Strain into the tall glass, top up with soda water and garnish with cucumber or lime slices.

BANANA DAIQUIRI

2 MEASURES WHITE RUM

½ MEASURE BANANA LIQUEUR

½ SMALL BANANA

½ MEASURE LIME CORDIAL

1 TSP ICING SUGAR & BANANA, TO GARNISH

Put some cracked ice into a Margarita glass or tall goblet.

Put the rum, banana liqueur, banana and lime cordial into a food processor or blender and blend for 30 seconds.

Pour into the glass and garnish with icing sugar and a banana slice.

23

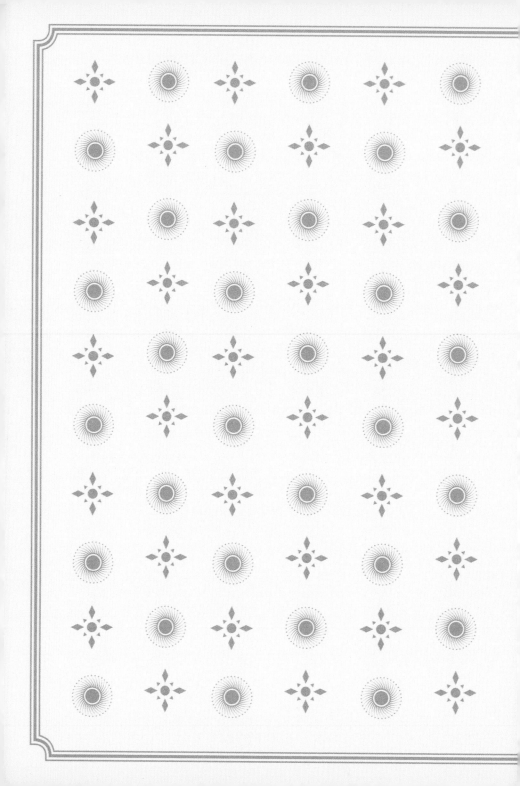

VIBRANT & ZESTY

STRAWBERRY DAIQUIRI

2 MEASURES GOLDEN RUM

2 MEASURES LIME JUICE

3 STRAWBERRIES, HULLED

DASH OF STRAWBERRY SYRUP

6 MINT LEAVES, PLUS A SPRIG, TO GARNISH

STRAWBERRY, TO GARNISH

Muddle the strawberries, syrup and mint leaves in the bottom of a cocktail shaker.

Add the rum and lime juice, shake with ice and double-strain into a chilled martini glass.

Garnish with a strawberry slice and a sprig of mint.

LIMON MOJITO

4 MEASURES LEMON BACARDI

2 LIMES, QUARTERED

4 TSP SOFT BROWN SUGAR

16 MINT LEAVES

SODA WATER, TO TOP

LEMON & LIME, TO GARNISH

Muddle the quarters of 2 limes with 4 teaspoons soft brown sugar and 16 mint leaves in the bottom of 2 highball glasses, then add 4 measures Limon Bacardi.

Stir and top up with soda water.

Garnish with lemon and lime slices and serve with straws.

BAJAN DAIQUIRI

2 MEASURES AMBER RUM

2 TSP CAMPARI

4 TSP LIME JUICE

3 TSP SUGAR SYRUP

1 MEASURE PINEAPPLE JUICE

LIME, TO GARNISH

Add some ice cubes and all the ingredients to a cocktail shaker.

Shake and strain into a martini glass and garnish with a lime wedge.

29

TAHITIAN MULE

1 MEASURE AMBER RUM

3 TSP ORANGE LIQUEUR

3 TSP GINGER BEER

2 TSP LIME JUICE

LIME & ORANGE, TO GARNISH

Fill a glass with ice and pour in the rum, lime juice, orange liqueur and ginger beer and stir.

Garnish with lime and orange slices.

PORT ANTONIO

3 MEASURES WHITE OR GOLDEN RUM

½ TSP GRENADINE

1 MEASURE LIME JUICE

LIME & COCKTAIL CHERRY, TO GARNISH

Spoon the grenadine into a chilled cocktail glass and put the ice cubes into a mixing glass.

Pour the lime juice and rum over the ice and stir vigorously, then strain into the cocktail glass.

Wrap a lime rind around the cherry, place them on a cocktail stick and use them to garnish the drink.

GAUGIN

2 MEASURES WHITE RUM

2 TSP PASSION FRUIT SYRUP

2 TSP LEMON JUICE

1 TSP LIME JUICE

COCKTAIL CHERRY, TO GARNISH

Put 3–4 measures crushed ice into a food processor or blender with all the ingredients and blend at low speed for 15 seconds.

Strain into a glass straight up and add a cocktail cherry to garnish.

GOLDEN APRICOT

3 TBSP RUM

3 TSP APRICOT LIQUEUR

4 TSP LIME JUICE

4 TSP SUGAR SYRUP

1 EGG YOLK

4 MEASURES SODA WATER

DRIED APRICOT, TO GARNISH

Put the rum, apricot liqueur, lime juice, sugar syrup and egg yolk into a food processor or blender and blend.

Strain into a glass, fill the glass with ice cubes and then top up with the soda water.

Garnish with a dried apricot.

APRICOT DAIQUIRI

1 MEASURE WHITE RUM

1 MEASURE LEMON JUICE

½ MEASURE APRICOT LIQUEUR OR BRANDY

3 RIPE APRICOTS, SKINNED & STONED

APRICOT, MINT SPRIG & COCKTAIL CHERRY,

TO GARNISH

Put some crushed ice into a food processor or blender.

Add all the ingredients and blend for 1 minute or until smooth.

Pour into a chilled cocktail glass and garnish with an apricot slice, cocktail cherry and mint sprig.

FROZEN MANGO
DAIQUIRI

CRUSHED ICE

½ MANGO, PEELED & STONED

1 MEASURE LIME JUICE

2 MEASURES WHITE RUM

1 TSP ICING SUGAR

MANGO, TO GARNISH

Put a small scoop of crushed ice into a food processor or blender.

Add all the ingredients and blend until smooth.

Serve in a chilled glass and garnish with mango slices.

RUM COLLINS

2 MEASURES WHITE RUM

1 TSP CASTER SUGAR

1 DASH ORANGE BITTERS

2 TSP LEMON JUICE

3 MEASURES SODA WATER

LEMON & ORANGE, TO GARNISH

Add the rum and sugar to a glass and stir until the sugar has dissolved. Then add the orange bitters and lemon juice.

Fill the glass with ice cubes, top up with the soda water, then stir.

Garnish with a lemon and orange wedge.

COCONUT DAIQUIRI

2 MEASURES WHITE RUM

1 MEASURE COCONUT LIQUEUR

2 MEASURES LIME JUICE

1 TSP GRENADINE

LIME, TO GARNISH

Put 4–5 crushed ice cubes into a cocktail shaker and pour over the remaining ingredients.

Shake until a frost forms and strain into a cocktail glass and garnish with a lime slice.

BLACK WIDOW

2 MEASURES DARK RUM

1 MEASURE SOUTHERN COMFORT

JUICE OF ½ LIME

1 DASH SUGAR SYRUP

LIME, TO GARNISH

Put some cracked ice into a tall glass.

Put the rum, Southern Comfort, lime juice and sugar syrup into a cocktail shaker. Shake lightly.

Strain into the glass and garnish with a lime slice.

41

CAPRISSIMA DE UVA

2 MEASURES AMBER RUM

2 TSP VELVET FALERNUM

½ LIME, PLUS EXTRA, TO GARNISH

5 RED GRAPES, PLUS EXTRA, TO GARNISH

2 TSP SUGAR

Muddle the lime and grapes at the base of a glass.

Add the rum, sugar and velvet falernum and half-fill the glass with crushed ice. Churn the mixture with a muddler until thoroughly mixed.

Top the glass up with more crushed ice and garnish with a lime wheel and a grape.

FROZEN MANGO & MINT SPICED DAIQUIRI

1 MEASURE LIME JUICE

2 TSP SUGAR SYRUP

2 MEASURES CAPTAIN MORGAN ORIGINAL SPICED RUM

½ RIPE MANGO, PEELED & ROUGHLY CHOPPED

6 MINT LEAVES

MANGO & MINT SPRIG, TO GARNISH

Put some crushed ice into a food processor or blender, add all the ingredients and blend until smooth.

Pour into a large Champagne saucer and garnish with a mango slice and mint sprig.

DISCOVERY BAY

3 DROPS ANGOSTURA BITTERS

JUICE OF ½ LIME

1 TSP CURAÇAO OR BLUE CURAÇAO

1 TSP SUGAR SYRUP

3 MEASURES GOLDEN OR DARK RUM

LIME, TO GARNISH

Put the ice cubes into a cocktail shaker, then shake the bitters over the ice.

Pour in the lime juice, Curaçao, sugar syrup and rum and shake until a frost forms.

Strain into an old-fashioned glass and garnish with lime slices.

DUKE'S DAIQUIRI

2 MEASURES WHITE RUM

3 TSP LIME JUICE

1 MEASURE SUGAR SYRUP

TINNED PEACH HALF, DRAINED

1 MEASURES CLOUDY APPLE JUICE

1 TSP GRENADINE

LIME & BLACK CHERRY, TO GARNISH

Add all ingredients to a food processor or blender and blend until smooth.

Pour into a glass, garnish with a lime wheel and a cherry.

47

MELON DAIQUIRI

2 MEASURES RUM

1 MEASURE LIME JUICE

½ MEASURE MIDORI

MELON, TO GARNISH

Add all the ingredients, plus some some crushed ice, to a cocktail shaker.

Shake and strain into a chilled martini glass and garnish with a small wedge of melon.

BOSSA NOVA

2 MEASURES WHITE RUM

½ MEASURE GALLIANO

½ MEASURE APRICOT BRANDY

4 MEASURES PRESSED APPLE JUICE

1 MEASURE LIME JUICE

½ MEASURE SUGAR SYRUP

LIME, TO GARNISH

Put some ice cubes into a cocktail shaker with the rum, Galliano, apricot brandy, fruit juices and sugar syrup and shake well.

Strain into a highball glass filled with ice cubes.

Garnish with split lime wedges and serve with long straws.

49

BAIJAN SWIZZLE

1 MEASURE WHITE RUM

3 TSP FALERNUM

4 TSP LIME JUICE

2 DASHES ANGOSTURA BITTERS

5 MINT LEAVES

MINT SPRING, TO GARNISH

Add all the ingredients to a sling glass half filled with crushed ice and swizzle the drink by spinning a bar spoon between the two flat palms of your hand.

Top the glass up with crushed ice, garnish with a mint sprig.

WRONG ISLAND SPICED TEA

1 MEASURE SPICED RUM

2 TSP APRICOT LIQUEUR

1 TSP GINGER JUICE

3 TSP LIME JUICE

3 TSP SUGAR SYRUP

2 DASHES ANGOSTURA BITTERS

1 YELLOW TEA BAG

CRYSTALLIZED GINGER, TO GARNISH

Add 1 yellow tea bag to a cup of boiling water and leave to cool.

Place the rest of the ingredients in a soda syphon and add 4 measures of the cooled yellow tea and charge with carbon dioxide, following the manufacturer's instructions.

Chill in the refrigerator before serving in an ice sling glass, garnished with crystallized ginger.

INTENSE & SULTRY

PINK MOJITO

1½ MEASURES WHITE RUM

½ MEASURE CHAMBORD

2 TSP SUGAR SYRUP

6 MINT LEAVES

½ LIME, CUT INTO WEDGES

3 RASPBERRIES

CRANBERRY JUICE, TO TOP

MINT SPRIG, TO GARNISH

Muddle the mint leaves, lime wedges, sugar syrup and raspberries in a highball glass. Add some crushed ice and the rum and Chambord.

Stir well, top up with cranberry juice and garnish with a mint sprig.

TOBAGO

½ MEASURE LOW-PROOF RUM

½ MEASURE GIN

1 TSP LIME JUICE

1 TSP GUAVA SYRUP

Put the rum, gin, lime juice and guava syrup into a cocktail shaker and shake well.

Pour into a glass over crushed ice.

RUM CRUSTA

2 MEASURES DARK RUM

1 MEASURE COINTREAU

2 TSP MARASCHINO LIQUEUR

2 TSP LIME JUICE

LIME WEDGE

CASTER SUGAR

2 GRAPES, TO GARNISH

Frost the rim of an old-fashioned glass by moistening it with the lime wedge and pressing it into the sugar.

Put some ice cubes into a cocktail shaker with the rum, Cointreau, Maraschino liqueur and lime juice and shake well.

Strain into an old-fashioned glass filled with crushed ice and garnish with the grapes.

BEAUTIFUL BETH

1 MEASURE LIGHT RUM

1 MEASURE MALIBU

½ MEASURE COINTREAU

CHILLED COLA, TO TOP

CHERRY, TO GARNISH (OPTIONAL)

Put some ice cubes into a cocktail shaker and pour the rum, Malibu and Cointreau over it.

Shake until a frost forms, strain into an old-fashioned glass and top up with chilled cola.

Garnish with a cherry, if liked.

ST LUCIA

2 MEASURES WHITE OR GOLDEN RUM

1 MEASURE CURAÇAO

1 MEASURE DRY VERMOUTH

1 TSP GRENADINE

JUICE OF ½ ORANGE

ORANGE & COCKTAIL CHERRY, TO GARNISH

Put 4–5 ice cubes into a cocktail shaker and pour over the Curaçao, vermouth, orange juice, grenadine and rum.

Shake until a frost forms, then pour without straining into a highball glass.

Garnish with an orange rind spiral and a cocktail cherry.

EL DORADO

1 MEASURE WHITE RUM

1 MEASURE ADVOCAAT

1 MEASURE CRÈME DE CACAO

2 TSP GRATED COCONUT

Put some ice cubes into a cocktail shaker.

Pour the rum, advocaat and crème de cacao over the ice and add the coconut.

Shake until a frost forms, then strain into a chilled cocktail glass.

CLEM THE CUBAN

1 MEASURE HAVANA CLUB 3-YEAR-OLD RUM

1 DASH APPLE SCHNAPPS

1 MINT SPRIG

2 LIME WEDGES

Muddle the schnapps, mint sprig and lime wedges in a cocktail shaker, then add the rum and a scoop of crushed ice.

Shake very briefly and double strain into a shot glass.

SERENADE

1 MEASURE WHITE RUM

½ MEASURE AMARETTO DI SARONNO LIQUEUR

½ MEASURE COCONUT CREAM

2 MEASURES PINEAPPLE JUICE

PINEAPPLE, TO GARNISH

Put a few ice cubes into a food processor or blender, add the rum, Amaretto di Saronno, coconut cream and pineapple juice and blend for 20 seconds.

Pour into a tall glass over 3 more ice cubes, garnish with a pineapple slice and serve with a straw.

ALMOND CIGAR

2 MEASURES HAVANA CLUB 3-YEAR-OLD RUM

1 MEASURE LIME CORDIAL

1 MEASURE AMARETTO DI SARONNO LIQUEUR

CINNAMON STICK & LIME, TO GARNISH

Pour the rum, lime cordial and Amaretto di Saronno into a chilled cocktail shaker.

Shake and strain into a chilled martini glass and garnish with a cinnamon stick and a lime rind twist.

RUM OLD FASHIONED

2 MEASURES WHITE RUM

½ MEASURE DARK RUM

1 DASH ANGOSTURA BITTERS

1 DASH LIME BITTERS

1 TSP CASTER SUGAR

½ MEASURE WATER

CHERRY, TO GARNISH

Stir 1 ice cube with the bitters, sugar and water in a heavy-based old-fashioned glass until the sugar has dissolved.

Add the white rum, stir and add the some more ice cubes.

Add the dark rum and stir once again.

Garnish with a cherry.

RUM
REFASHIONED

2 MEASURES AGED RUM

4 DASHES ANGOSTURA BITTERS

1 BROWN SUGAR CUBE

SUGAR SYRUP

LIME, TO GARNISH

Put the sugar cube into an old-fashioned glass, then splash in the bitters, add 2 ice cubes and stir.

Add a quarter of the rum and another 2 ice cubes and stir.

Continue building, and stirring, with the rum and ice cubes, adding sugar syrup to taste.

Garnish with a lime rind twist.

FIRST THE MONEY

1 MEASURE DARK RUM

1 TSP WHITE CRÈME DE MENTHE

¾ MEASURE COFFEE LIQUEUR

1 LIME

COLA, TO TOP

Cut the lime into wedges and muddle with the crème de menthe in a highball glass.

Fill the glass with crushed ice and add the rum and Toussaint.

Top up with cola.

PINK ANGEL

½ MEASURE WHITE RUM

¼ MEASURE ADVOCAAT

¼ MEASURE CHERRY BRANDY

1 EGG WHITE

½ MEASURE DOUBLE CREAM

Put some ice cubes into a cocktail shaker with the rum, advocaat, cherry brandy, egg white and cream and shake well.

Strain into a cocktail glass.

WHITE WITCH

1 MEASURE WHITE RUM

½ MEASURE WHITE CRÈME DE CACAO

½ MEASURE COINTREAU

JUICE OF ½ LIME

SODA WATER, TO TOP

ORANGE & LIME, TO GARNISH

Put some ice cubes into a cocktail shaker and pour over the rum, crème de cacao, Cointreau and lime juice.

Shake and strain over 4 ice cubes in an old-fashioned glass.

Top up with soda water, stir to mix and garnish with orange and lime slices. Serve with straws.

71

THE BODAS COCKTAIL

1 MEASURE WHITE RUM

1 MEASURE RED DUBONNET

1 MEASURE ORANGE CURAÇAO

COCKTAIL CHERRIES, TO GARNISH

Pour the rum, Dubonnet and Curaçao into a mixing glass and stir well.

Put into a small martini glass and decorate with cocktail cherries on cocktail sticks.

HUMMINGBIRD

1 MEASURE DARK RUM

1 MEASURE LIGHT RUM

1 MEASURE SOUTHERN COMFORT

1 MEASURE ORANGE JUICE

COLA, TO TOP

ORANGE, TO GARNISH

Put some crushed ice into a cocktail shaker and pour the rums, Southern Comfort and orange juice over it.

Shake until a frost forms, strain into a long glass and top up with cola.

Garnish with an orange slice and serve with a straw.

TIKI TREAT

2 MEASURES AGED RUM

1 DASH LEMON JUICE

1 TSP CASTER SUGAR

½ RIPE MANGO, PEELED AND STONED, PLUS

EXTRA SLICES, TO GARNISH

3 COCONUT CHUNKS

1 MEASURE COCONUT CREAM

Put a small scoop of crushed ice into a food processor or blender with all the other ingredients and blend until smooth.

Serve in a stemmed hurricane glass with long straws and garnish with mango slices.

75

BATISE

1 MEASURE GRAND MARNIER

2 MEASURES GOLDEN OR DARK RUM

Put 4–5 ice cubes into a mixing glass.

Pour the Grand Marnier and rum over the ice, stir vigorously, then strain into a cocktail glass.

HAWAIIAN DELUXE

1½ MEASURES COCONUT RUM

½ MEASURE COINTREAU

½ MEASURE AGED RUM

1 MEASURE COCONUT CREAM

2 MEASURES PINEAPPLE JUICE

1 DASH SUGAR SYRUP

1 DASH LEMON JUICE

1 DASH GRENADINE

PINEAPPLE & COCONUT, TO GARNISH

Put some ice cubes into a cocktail shaker with all the other ingredients, except the grenadine. Shake well.

Strain into a large hurricane glass.

Drizzle the grenadine over the drink and garnish with pineapple and coconut wedges. Serve with long straws.

HAVANA ZOMBIE

1 MEASURE WHITE RUM

1 MEASURE GOLDEN RUM

1 MEASURE DARK RUM

JUICE OF 1 LIME

5 TBSP PINEAPPLE JUICE

1 TSP SUGAR SYRUP

LIME, TO GARNISH

Put 4–5 ice cubes into a mixing glass.

Pour the fruit juices, sugar syrup and rums over the ice and stir vigorously.

Pour without straining into a tall glass and garnish with a lime wheel.

JOLLY ROGER

1 MEASURE DARK RUM

1 MEASURE GALLIANO

½ MEASURE APRICOT BRANDY

3 MEASURES ORANGE JUICE

APRICOT, ORANGE & LEMON, TO GARNISH

Put some cracked ice into a cocktail shaker with the rum, Galliano, apricot brandy and orange juice and shake well.

Strain into a tall glass over a few more cracked ice cubes.

Garnish with apricot, orange & lemon slices.

CAPRISSIMA DA FRAMOESA

2 MEASURES AMBER RUM

2 TSP RASPBERRY LIQUEUR

1 TSP PASTIS

½ LIME

5 RASPBERRIES

2 PINK GRAPEFRUIT SLICES

3 TSP SUGAR SYRUP

PINK GRAPEFRUIT & RASPBERRY, TO GARNISH

Muddle ½ lime, 5 raspberries and 1 teaspoon pastis in a collins glass.

Add the remaining ingredients and half-fill the glass with crushed ice. Churn with a muddler until thoroughly mixed.

Top up the glass with more crushed ice, garnish with a raspberry and a pink grapefruit wedge.

RUDE JUDE

1 MEASURE WHITE RUM

1 DASH STRAWBERRY PURÉE

1 DASH STRAWBERRY SYRUP

1 DASH LIME JUICE

Put some ice cubes into a cocktail shaker and pour over the rum, strawberry purée, strawberry syrup and lime juice.

Shake well and strain into a shot glass.

KINKY WITCH

1 MEASURE HAVANA CLUB 3-YEAR-OLD RUM

1 MEASURE HAVANA CLUB SILVER DRY RUM

2 TSP OVER-PROOF RUM

½ MEASURE ORANGE CURAÇAO

½ MEASURE CRÈME DE MURE

½ MEASURE ORGEAT SYRUP

2 MEASURES ORANGE JUICE

2 MEASURES GRAPEFRUIT JUICE

GRAPEFRUIT, TO GARNISH

Put some ice cubes into a cocktail shaker with the Havana Club rums, Curaçao, crème de mure, orgeat syrup and fruit juices and shake well.

Strain into a highball glass filled with ice cubes, float the over-proof rum on top and garnish with grapefruit wedges.

SHARERS & PUNCHES

PIÑA COCO

4 MEASURES AMBER RUM

1 MEASURE GALLIANO

1 MEASURE COCONUT CREAM

4 MEASURES PASSION FRUIT JUICE

1 PINEAPPLE

1 BANANA

Cut the top off the pineapple and use a pineapple corer to remove the flesh inside the pineapple. Set aside the hollowed-out pineapple.

Cut the pineapple flesh into chunks.

Add 7 chunks of the pineapple and the remaining ingredients to a food processor or blender and blend until smooth.

Pour into the hollowed-out pineapple and serve with straws.

PLANTER'S PUNCH

**4 MEASURES MYER'S JAMAICAN PLANTER'S
PUNCH RUM**

8 DROPS ANGOSTURA BITTERS

1 MEASURE LIME JUICE

4 MEASURES CHILLED WATER

2 MEASURES SUGAR SYRUP

ORANGE & LIME, TO GARNISH

Put the rum, bitters, lime juice,
water and sugar syrup in a cocktail
shaker and add some ice cubes.

Shake and strain into 2 chilled
glasses and garnish with orange
and lime slices.

TEMPO

1 MEASURE WHITE RUM

1 MEASURE LIME JUICE

½ MEASURE CRÉME DE CACAO

1 DASH ANGOSTURA BITTERS

LEMONADE, TO TOP

LIME, TO GARNISH

Put 3 cracked ice cubes into each of 2 chilled highball glasses and pour 1 measure white rum, 1 measure lime juice and ½ measure crème de cacao into each glass.

Add a dash of Angostura bitters, stir and top up with lemonade.

Garnish with lime slices.

LOLA'S PUNCH

4 MEASURES WHITE RUM

3 MEASURES LEMON JUICE

3 MEASURES SUGAR SYRUP

3 MEASURES APPLE JUICE

3 MEASURES MANGO JUICE

200 ML WHITE WINE

250 ML SODA WATER

MANGO & APPLE, TO GARNISH

Fill a jug with ice cubes, add all the ingredient and stir.

Garnish with mango and apple slices.

COLONIAL PUNCH

200 ML PINEAPPLE & CHERRY-INFUSED RUM

(SEE PAGE 115)

2 MEASURES LEMON JUICE

2 MEASURES SUGAR SYRUP

4 MEASURES PINEAPPLE JUICE

250 ML SPARKLING WINE

PINEAPPLE, TO GARNISH

Add all the ingredients to a large jug full of ice cubes and stir.

Garnish with pineapple wedges.

RUM PUNCH

200 ML SPICED RUM

4 MEASURES LIME JUICE

4 MEASURES SUGAR SYRUP

6 MEASURES PASSION FRUIT JUICE

6 MEASURES PINEAPPLE JUICE

6 MEASURES ORANGE JUICE

ORANGE, LIME & PASSION FRUIT, TO GARNISH

Fill a large jug with ice cubes, add all the ingredients and stir.

Garnish with orange and lime slices and passion fruit halves.

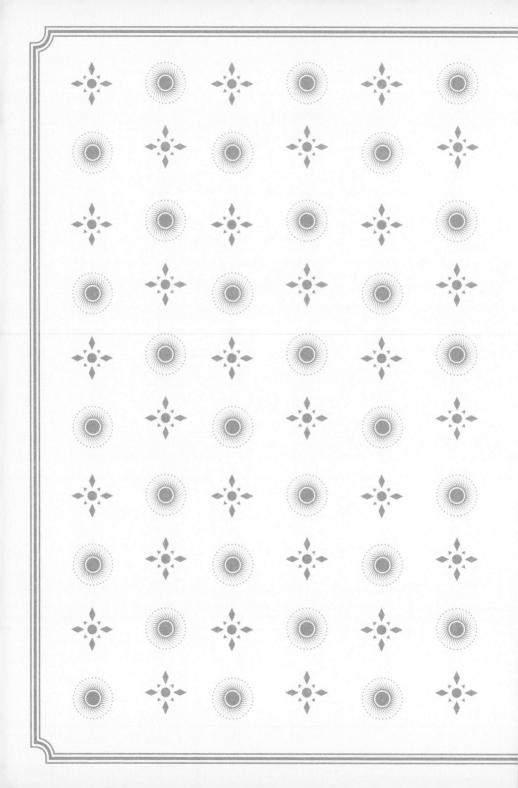

CLASSICS

DAIQUIRI

2 MEASURES LIGHT RUM

1 MEASURE SUGAR SYRUP

1 MEASURE LIME JUICE

LIME, TO GARNISH

Add all the ingredients, plus some ice cubes, to a cocktail shaker.

Shake and strain into a glass and garnish with a lime wedge.

MAI TAI

2 MEASURES GOLDEN RUM

2 TSP WOOD'S NAVY RUM

½ MEASURE ORANGE CURAÇAO

½ MEASURE ORGEAT SYRUP

JUICE OF 1 LIME

LIME & MINT SPRIG, TO GARNISH

Put some ice cubes into a cocktail shaker with the golden rum, Curaçao, orgeat syrup and lime juice and shake well.

Strain over crushed ice into an old-fashioned glass, float the Navy rum on top and garnish with lime rind and a mint sprig.

HURRICANE

1 MEASURE WHITE RUM

1 MEASURE GOLDEN RUM

2 TSP PASSION FRUIT SYRUP

2 TSP LIME JUICE

Put some ice cubes into a cocktail shaker and pour over the rums, passion fruit syrup and lime juice.

Shake well and strain into a cocktail glass and add ice cubes.

MOJITO

5 MEASURES WHITE RUM

16 MINT LEAVES, PLUS SPRIGS, TO GARNISH

1 LIME, CUT INTO WEDGES

4 TSP CANE SUGAR

SODA WATER, TO TOP

Muddle the mint leaves, lime and sugar in the bottom of 2 highball glasses and fill with crushed ice.

Add the rum, stir and top up with soda water.

Garnish with mint sprigs and serve with straws.

LONG ISLAND ICED TEA

1 MEASURE WHITE RUM

1 MEASURE VODKA

1 MEASURE GIN

1 MEASURE TEQUILA

1 MEASURE COINTREAU

1 MEASURE LEMON JUICE

COLA, TO TOP

LEMON, TO GARNISH

Put the rum, vodka, gin, tequila, Cointreau and lemon juice in a cocktail shaker with some ice cubes and shake to mix.

Strain into 2 highball glasses filled with ice cubes and top up with cola.

Garnish with lemon slices.

CUBA LIBRE

4 MEASURES GOLDEN RUM

JUICE OF 1 LIME

COLA, TO TOP

LIME, TO GRANISH

Fill 2 highball glasses with ice cubes.
Pour over the rum and lime juice
and stir.

Top up with cola, garnish with lime
wedges and serve with straws.

103

THE PAPA DOBLE

3 MEASURES WHITE RUM

½ MEASURE MARASCHINO LIQUEUR

1 MEASURE LIME JUICE

1½ MEASURES GRAPEFRUIT JUICE

GRAPEFRUIT, TO GARNISH

Put a scoop of crushed ice into a food processor or blender with the rum, Maraschino liqueur and fruit juices and blend until smooth.

Serve in a highball glass with grapefruit slices.

PIÑA COLADA

1 MEASURE WHITE RUM

2 MEASURES COCONUT MILK

2 MEASURES PINEAPPLE JUICE

PINEAPPLE, TO GARNISH

Put some cracked ice into a cocktail shaker, with the rum, coconut milk and pineapple juice.

Shake lightly to mix and strain into a large glass and garnish with the pineapple wedge.

Serve with long straws.

ZOMBIE

1 MEASURE DARK RUM

1 MEASURE WHITE RUM

½ MEASURE GOLDEN RUM

2 TSP OVER-PROOF RUM

½ MEASURE APRICOT BRANDY

JUICE OF ½ LIME

1 TSP GRENADINE

2 MEASURES PINEAPPLE JUICE

½ MEASURE SUGAR SYRUP

PINEAPPLE WEDGE & LEAF & SUGAR, TO GARNISH

Put some ice cubes into a cocktail shaker with the dark, white and golden rums, apricot brandy, lime juice, grenadine, pineapple juice and sugar syrup and shake well.

Pour without straining into a chilled glass and float the over-proof rum on top.

Garnish with a pineapple wedge and leaf, and sprinkle a pinch of sugar over the top.

EGG NOG

2 MEASURES RUM

6 MEASURES MILK

1 EGG

1 TBSP SUGAR SYRUP

NUTMEG & CINNAMON STICK, TO GARNISH

Half-fill a cocktail shaker with ice cubes. Add the egg, sugar syrup, rum and milk and shake well for about 1 minute.

Strain into a tumbler and sprinkle with a little grated nutmeg and garnish with a cinnamon stick.

RED RUM

2 MEASURES BACARDI 8-YEAR-OLD RUM

½ MEASURE SLOE GIN

SMALL HANDFUL OF REDCURRANTS

½ MEASURE LEMON JUICE

½ MEASURE VANILLA SYRUP

REDCURRANT STRING, TO GARNISH

Muddle the redcurrants and sloe gin in a cocktail shaker.

Add some ice cubes with the remaining ingredients and shake well.

Double strain into a chilled martini glass and garnish with a redcurrant string.

TIPS & TECHNIQUES FOR CRAFTING THE PERFECT COCKTAIL

WHAT MAKES A GOOD COCKTAIL?

Good cocktails, like good food, are based around quality ingredients. As with cooking, using fresh and homemade ingredients can often make the huge difference between a good drink and an outstanding drink. All of this can be found in department stores, online or in kitchen shops.

COCKTAIL INGREDIENTS

ICE This is a key part of cocktails and you'll need lots of it. Purchase it from your supermarket or freeze big tubs of water, then crack this up to use in your drinks. If you're hosting a big party and want to serve some punches, which will need lots of ice, it may be worthwhile finding if you have a local ice supplier that supplies catering companies, as this can be much more cost effective.

CITRUS JUICE It's important to use fresh citrus juice in your drinks; bottled versions taste awful and will not produce good drinks. Store your fruit out of the refrigerator at room temperature. Look for a soft-skinned fruit for juicing, which you can do with a juicer or citrus press. You can keep fresh citrus juice for a couple of days in the refrigerator, sealed to prevent oxidation.

SUGAR SYRUP You can buy sugar syrup or you can make your own. The most basic form of sugar syrup is made by mixing caster sugar and hot water together, and stirring until the sugar has dissolved. The key when preparing sugar syrups is to use a 1:1 ratio of sugar to liquid. White sugar acts as a flavour enhancer, while dark sugars have unique, more toffee flavours and work well with dark spirits.

BASIC SUGAR SYRUP RECIPE
(Makes 1 litre (1¾ pints) of sugar syrup)
Dissolve 1 kg (2 lb) caster sugar in 1 litre (1¾ pints) of hot water.
Allow to cool.
Sugar syrup will keep in a sterilized bottle stored in the refrigerator for up to 2 weeks.

PINEAPPLE & CHERRY-INFUSED RUM
Add ¼ large pineapple, peeled and cubed, 1 tablespoon maraschino cherries and 500 ml white rum to a jug and leave to infuse for at least 5 days before use.

CHOOSING GLASSWARE

There are many different cocktails, but they all fall into one of three categories: long, short or shot. Long drinks generally have more mixer than alcohol, often served with ice and a straw. The terms 'straight up' and 'on the rocks' are synonymous with the short drink, which tends to be more about the spirit, often combined with a single mixer at most. Finally, there is the shot which is made up mainly from spirits and liqueurs, designed to give a quick hit of alcohol. Glasses are tailored to the type of drinks they will contain.

CHAMPAGNE FLUTE Used for Champagne or Champagne cocktails, the narrow mouth of the flute helps the drink to stay fizzy.

CHAMPAGNE SAUCER A classic glass, but not very practical for serving Champagne as the drink quickly loses its fizz.

MARGARITA OR COUPETTE GLASS When used for a Margarita, the rim is dipped in salt. Also used for daiquiris and other fruit-based cocktails.

HIGHBALL GLASS Suitable for any long cocktail, such as a Long Island Iced Tea.

COLLINS GLASS This is similar to a highball glass but is slightly narrower.

WINE GLASS Sangria is often served in one, but they are not usually used for cocktails.

OLD-FASHIONED GLASS Also known as a rocks glass, this is great for any drink that's served on the rocks or straight up.

SHOT GLASS Often found in two sizes — for a single or double measure. They are ideal for a single mouthful.

BALLOON GLASS Often used for fine spirits. The glass can be warmed to encourage the release of the drink's aroma.

HURRICANE GLASS Mostly found in beach bars, used for creamy, rum-based drinks.

BOSTON GLASS Often used by bartenders for mixing cocktails, good for fruity drinks.

TODDY GLASS A toddy glass is generally used for a hot drink, such as Irish Coffee.

SLING GLASS This has a very short stemmed base and is most famously used for a Singapore Sling.

MARTINI GLASS Also known as a cocktail glass, its thin neck design makes sure your hand can't warm the glass, or the cocktail.

USEFUL EQUIPMENT

Some pieces of equipment, such as shakers and the correct glasses, are vital for any cocktail party, while others, like ice buckets, can be obtained at a later date if needed. Below is a wishlist for anyone who wants to make cocktails on a regular basis.

SHAKER The Boston shaker is the most simple option, but it needs to be used in conjunction with a hawthorne strainer. Alternatively you could choose a shaker with a built-in strainer.

MEASURE OR JIGGER Single and double measures are available and are essential when you are mixing ingredients so that the proportions are always the same. One measure is 25 ml or 1 fl oz.

MIXING GLASS A mixing glass is used for those drinks that require only a gentle stirring before they are poured or strained.

HAWTHORNE STRAINER This type of strainer is often used in conjunction with a Boston shaker, but a simple tea strainer will also work well.

BAR SPOON Similar to a teaspoon but with a long handle, a bar spoon is used for stirring, layering and muddling drinks.

MUDDLING STICK Similar to a pestle, which will work just as well, a muddling stick, or muddler, is used to crush fruit or herbs in a glass or shaker for drinks like the Mojito.

BOTTLE OPENER Choose a bottle opener with two attachments, one for metal-topped bottles and a corkscrew for wine bottles.

POURERS A pourer is inserted into the top of a spirit bottle to enable the spirit to flow in a controlled manner.

FOOD PROCESSOR A food processor or blender is useful for making frozen cocktails and smoothies.

EQUIPMENT FOR GARNISHING Many drinks are garnished with fruit on cocktail sticks and these are available in wood, plastic or glass. Exotic drinks may be prettified with a paper umbrella and several long drinks are served with straws or swizzle sticks.

TECHNIQUES

With just a few basic techniques, your bartending skills will be complete. Follow the instructions to hone your craft.

BLENDING Frozen cocktails and smoothies are blended with ice in a blender until they are of a smooth consistency. Be careful not to add too much ice as this will dilute the cocktail. It's best to add a little at a time.

SHAKING The best-known cocktail technique and probably the most common. Used to mix ingredients thoroughly and quickly, and to chill the drink before serving.
1 Half-fill a cocktail shaker with ice cubes, or cracked or crushed ice.
2 If the recipe calls for a chilled glass add a few ice cubes and some cold water to the glass, swirl it around and discard.
3 Add the ingredients to the shaker and shake until a frost forms on the outside.
4 Strain the cocktail into the glass and serve.

MUDDLING A technique used to bring out the flavours of herbs and fruit using a blunt tool called a muddler.
1 Add chosen herb(s) to a highball glass. Add some sugar syrup and some lime wedges.
2 Hold the glass firmly and use a muddler or pestle to twist and press down.

3 Continue for 30 seconds, top up with crushed ice and add remaining ingredients.

DOUBLE-STRAINING To prevent all traces of puréed fruit and ice fragments from entering the glass, use a shaker with a built-in strainer in conjunction with a hawthorne strainer. A fine strainer also works well.

LAYERING Some spirits can be served layered on top of each other, causing 'lighter' spirits to float on top of your cocktail.
1 Pour the first ingredient into a glass, taking care that it does not touch the sides.
2 Position a bar spoon in the centre of the glass, rounded part down and facing you. Rest the spoon against the side of the glass as your pour the second ingredient down the spoon. It should float on top of the first liquid.
3 Repeat with the third ingredient, then carefully remove the spoon.

STIRRING Used when the ingredients need to be mixed and chilled, but also maintain their clarity. This ensures there are no ice fragments or air bubbles throughout the drink. Some cocktails require the ingredients to be prepared in a mixing glass, then strained into the serving glass.
1 Add ingredients to a glass, in recipe order.
2 Use a bar spoon to stir the drink, lightly or vigorously, as described in the recipe.
3 Finish the drink with any decoration and serve.

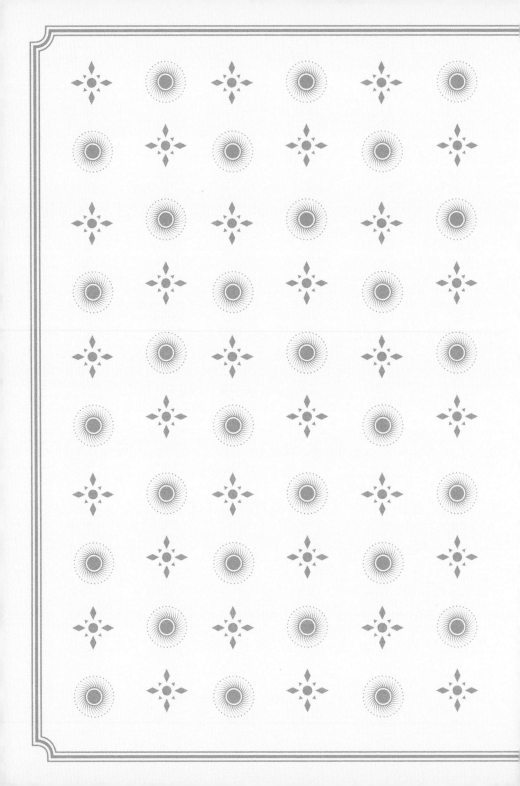

PICTURE CREDITS